001 002

003 004 005

001. Cuirassier, 1645. 002. Edward VI. 003, 005. Tilting lances, 16th century. 004. Henry I and General Gautier Von der Hoye.

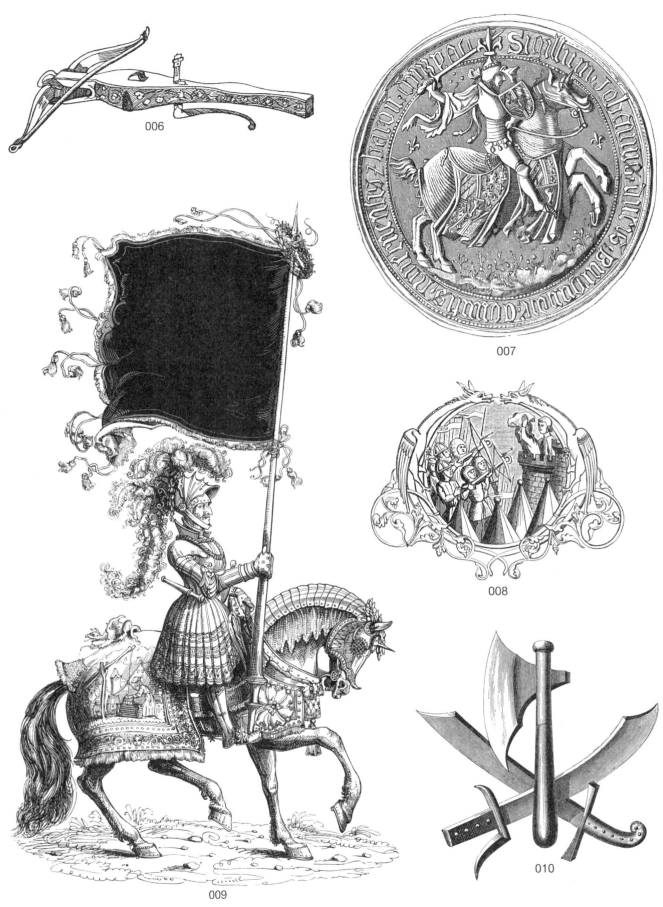

006. Crossbow, 13th century. 007. Seal of John, Duke of Burgundy, 1371–1419. 008. Assault on a fortified place, 13th century. 009. Knight. 010. Various arms, 15th century.

011. Ancient statue of Guy. **012.** Knight in his hauberk. **013.** William Longespee, Earl of Salisbury. **014.** Richard II. **015.** Degradation of a knight, 1565. **016.** Richard III.

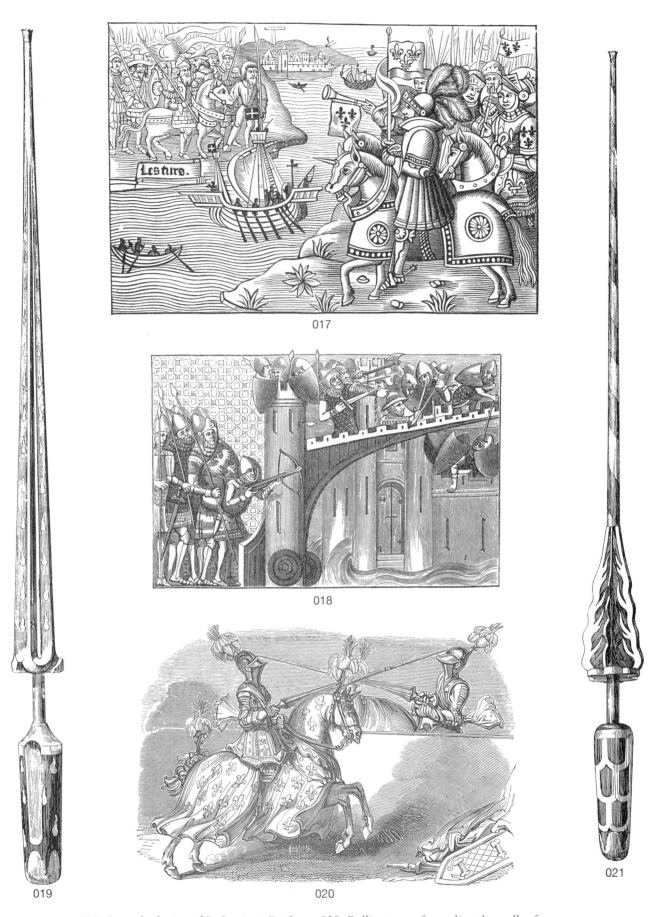

017. Disembarkation of St. Louis at Carthage. 018. Rolling tower for scaling the walls of towns, 14th century. 019, 021. Tilting lances, 16th century. 020. Tournament.

022. Melée. 023. Frankish warrior, 12th century. 024. Morning-star mace, 15th century.
025. German axe with gun in the handle, 1393. 026. Foot soldier, 1540. 027. Edward I.

028. Armor, 15th century. 029. French helmet, 15th century. 030. Edward, Prince of Wales. 031. Armor, 12th century. 032. St. George, patron of warriors, vanquishing the dragon.

033. Great seal of James I. **034.** Great seal of Henry III. **035.** Knights. **036.** Suit of very long-breasted armor. **037.** Helmet, 1645. **038.** Single combat to be decided by the judgment of God, 15th century.

039. Helmet. **040.** Geoffrey Plantagenet. **041.** Montacute, Earl of Salisbury. **042.** German sword, 14th century. **043.** Champion of the tournament, 15th century. **044.** German boar spear, 15th century.

045

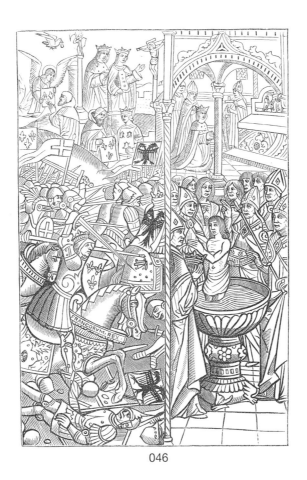

046

047

048

045. Tournament armor, 1586. **046.** Battle of Tolbiac and baptism of King Clovis.
047. Knight. **048.** Disembarkation of the crusaders at Damietta.

049. French gauntlet, 15th century. 050. French knight outfitted for a tournament, 16th century.

10

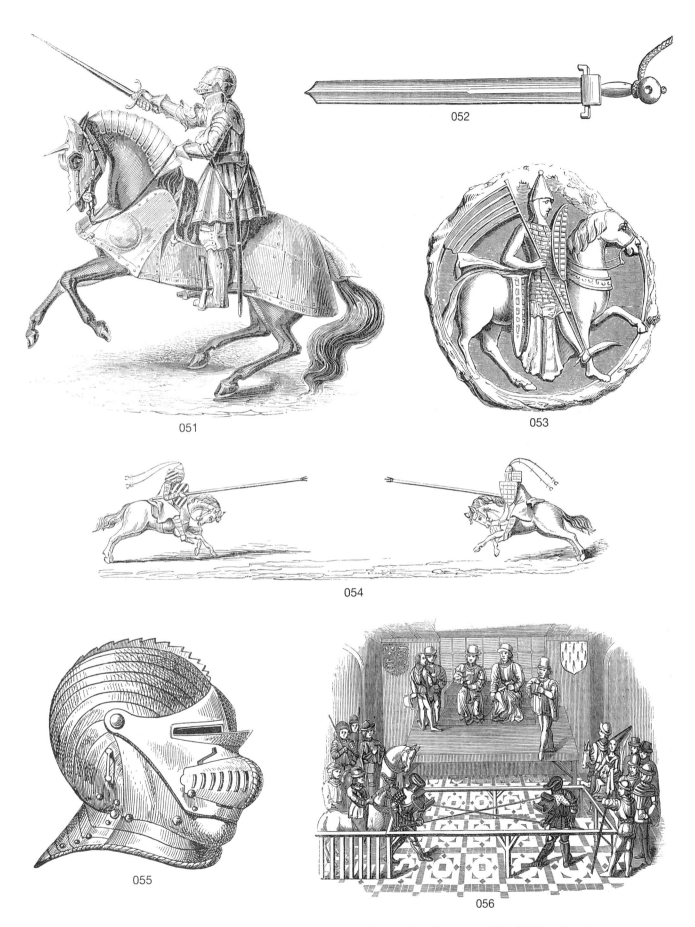

051. Henry VIII. **052.** Sword, 15th century. **053.** Tegulated armor. **054.** Knights jousting.
055. French helmet, 15th century. **056.** Tilting match, Nich. Clifford and J. Boucmell.

057

058

059

060

057. Great seal of Charles. **058.** Charles I. **059.** German knight, 15th century. **060.** Godefroy de Bouillon.

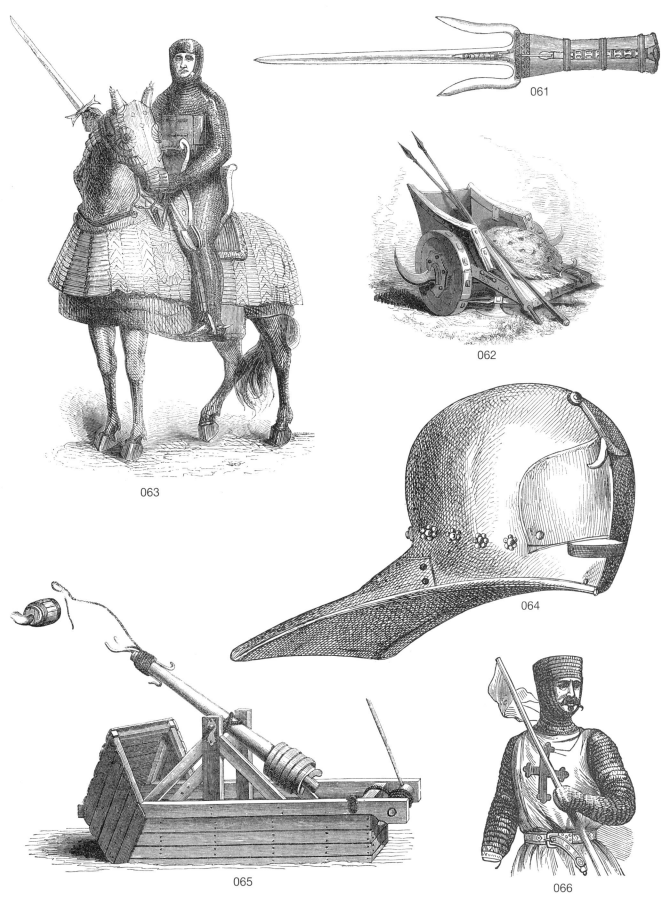

061. Moorish arm. 062. British war chariot, shield, and spears. 063. Norman crusader.
064. French helmet, 15th century. 065. Catapult. 066. Knight Templar, 13th century.

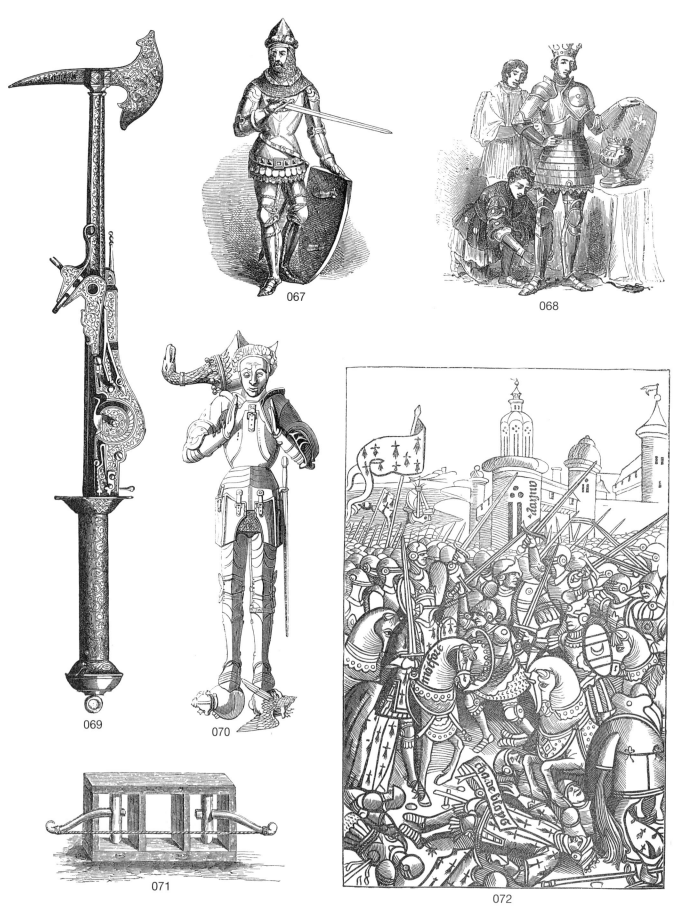

067. Earl of Westmoreland. 068. Henry V being armed by his esquires. 069. Battle-axe and pistol, 16th century. 070. Effigy of Richard Beauchamp, Earl of Warwick. 071. Ballista. 072. Battle of Auray.

073. French helmet, 15th century. 074. Bertrand du Guesclin at the tournament. 075. Armor, 15th century. 076. Great seal of Richard III. 077. Foot soldier, 1508. 078. Edward IV.

079. Coque, 15th century. 080. Arquebus. 081. Tournament helmet screwed on the breast-plate, 15th century. 082. Entry of Henry V into London. 083. Sword, 15th century. 084. Arms and costume of an Anglo-Saxon king and armor bearer. 085. Great seal of Edward I.

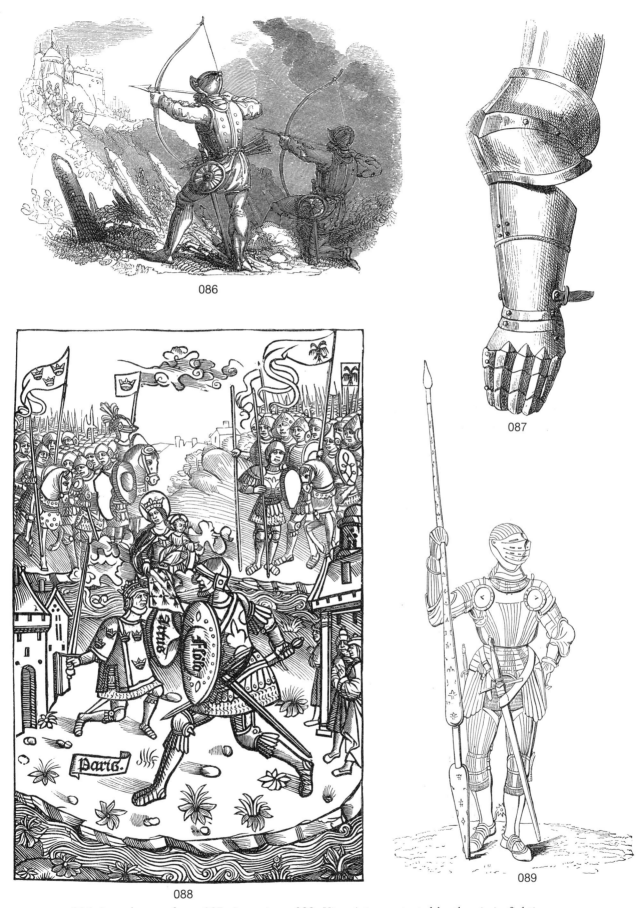

086. Long-bow archers. 087. Arm piece. 088. King Artus protected by the virgin fighting a giant, 1514. 089. Suit of fluted cap-a-pie armor.

090. Moorish arm, 11th–14th century. 091. Holy Roman Empire battle scene, 11th century.
092. Armor, 10th century. 093. "How both parties are out of their tents, armed and ready to do
their duty at the signal from the marshal, who has thrown the glove," 15th century.

094. Trellised armor, 9th century. 095. Ailette, 13th century. 096. French basinet, 14th century. 097. King John. 098. Suit of black armor, knight of St. George. 099. Mace. 100. Great seal of Richard II. 101. Richard II and Bolingbroke arrived at London. 102. William Marshall, Earl of Pembroke.

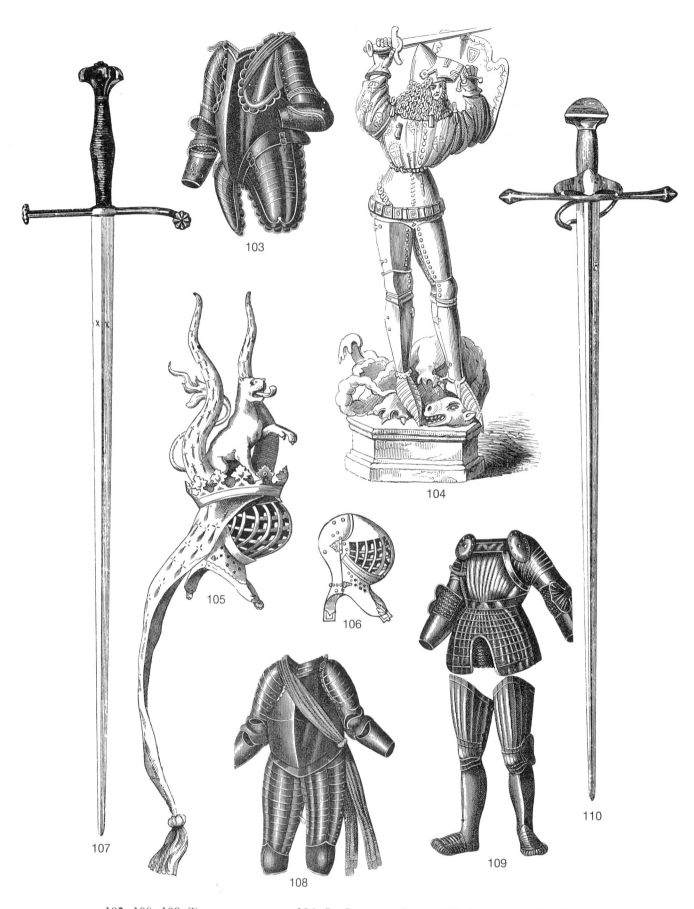

103, 108, 109. Tournament armor. 104. St. George at Dijon. 105. Tournament headdress. 106. Helmet. 107. German sword with square blade and black hilt, 15th century. 110. Saxon sword with short handle and flat pommel, 14th century.

111. Belt and pouch. 112. German warrior. 113. Chivalry represented by allegorical figures, 1573.
114. King Henry II wounded by Montgomery in a tournament, 1559. 115. Frankish warrior, 9th century.

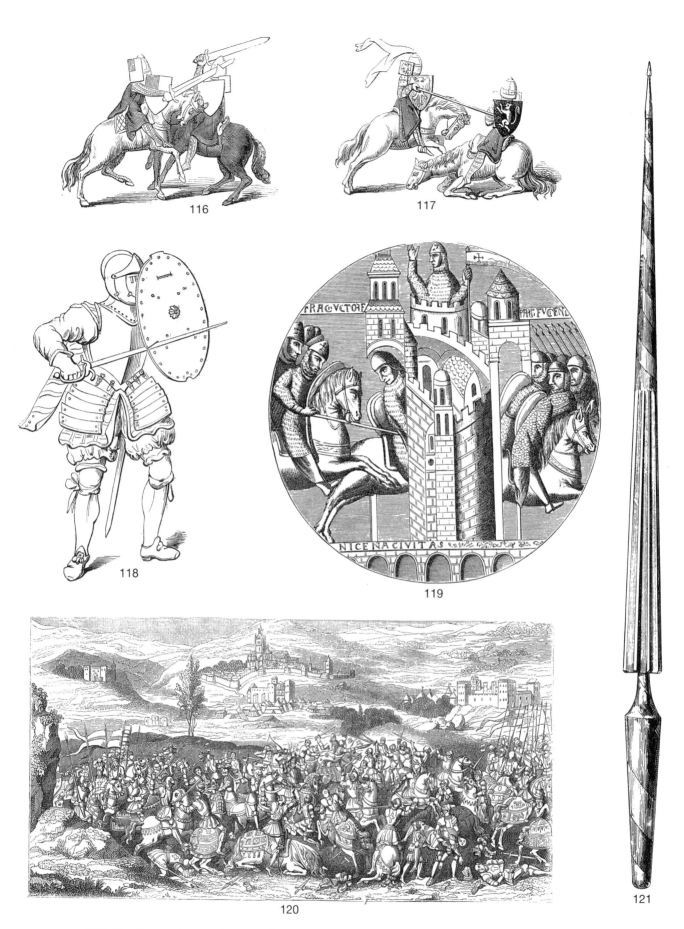

116. Knights combating. **117.** Knight jousting. **118.** Infantry armor, 1625. **119.** Taking of Nicaea by the crusaders, 12th century. **120.** Battle of the Spurs. **121.** Tilting lance, 16th century.

122. French casque, 15th century. 123. Watch. 124. Henry V. 125. St. Louis and his two brothers made prisoners by the Saracens. 126. Henry VII.

127. Gambeson, 14th century. 128. Banners used in the Battle of Agincourt. 129. Pavise, 14th century. 130. Battle scene. 131. Great seal of Edward IV. 132. Knight wielding a battle-axe. 133. Military costume, 6th–10th century.

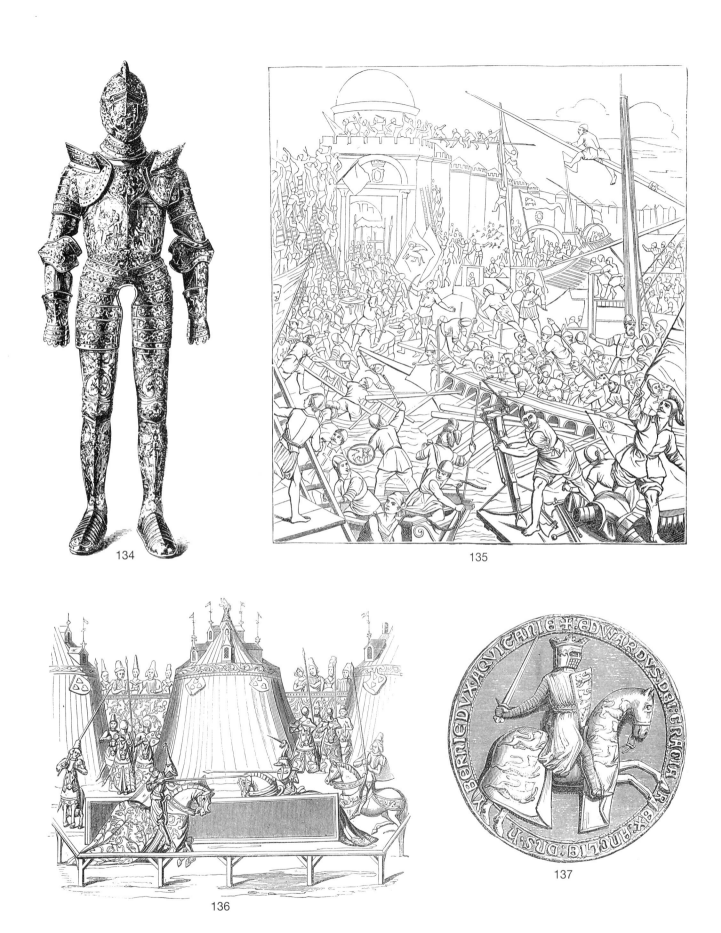

134. Armor worn by Henry II of England. **135.** Second taking of Constantinople.
136. Tournament. **137.** Great seal of Edward I.

138. Methods of attacking a wall, 11th century. **139.** Cannons, 15th century. **140.** Great seal of Henry IV. **141.** Knights and men-at-arms, 12th century. **142.** Scale armor. **143.** English ships of war, 15th century.

144. Bertrand du Guesclin fully armed. **145.** English knight's sword, 14th century.
146. Man-of-war, 1520. **147.** German sword, 15th century.

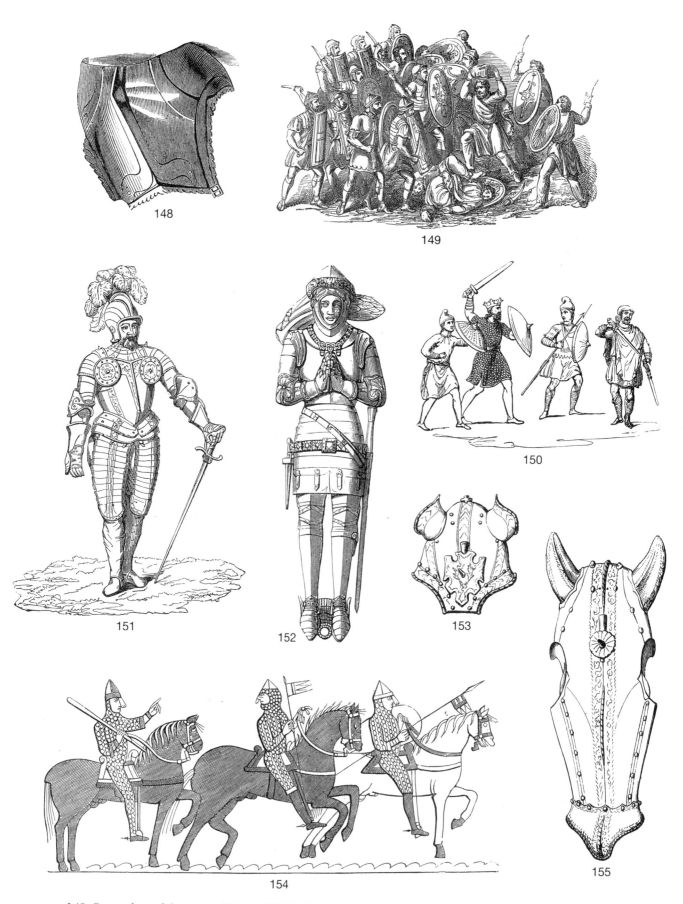

148. Breastplate of the time of Henry VIII. 149. Conflict between Romans and Barbarians. 150. Military habits of the Anglo-Saxons. 151. Suit of demi-lancer's armor. 152. Effigy of Sir Robert Grushill. 153, 155. Various English champfreins. 154. Duke William addressing his soldiers at the Field of Hastings.

156. Messenger bringing a letter to the king's army, 13th century. **157.** Aventaile. **158.** Henry, Prince of Wales. **159.** Fire arrow, 14th century. **160.** Knight. **161.** After the Battle of Hastings. **162.** John Howard, first duke of Norfolk.

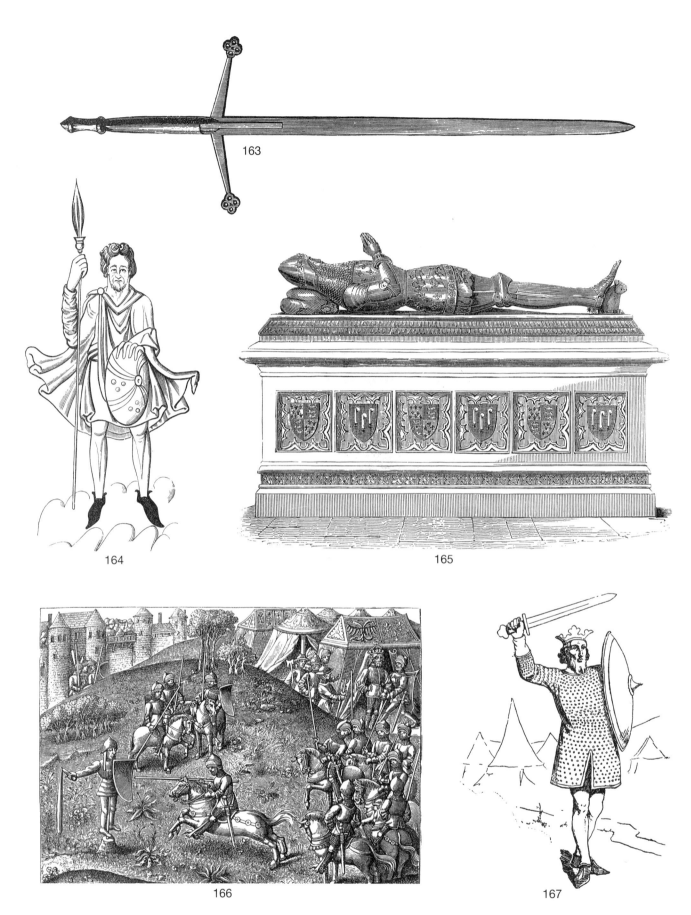

163. Medieval two-handed sword. 164. Costume of German soldiers, 6th–12th century. 165. Monument of Edward the Black Prince in Canterbury Cathedral. 166. Game of Quintain, 15th century. 167. English king, 8th century.

168. Knights. 169, 170. Tournament helmets. 171. Prize of the tournaments, 13th century. 172. Armor, 11th century.

173. Richard III. 174. Sword and dagger of James IV and two knights' banners. 175. Catapult.
176. Knight and the squire. 177. Great seal of Charles II.

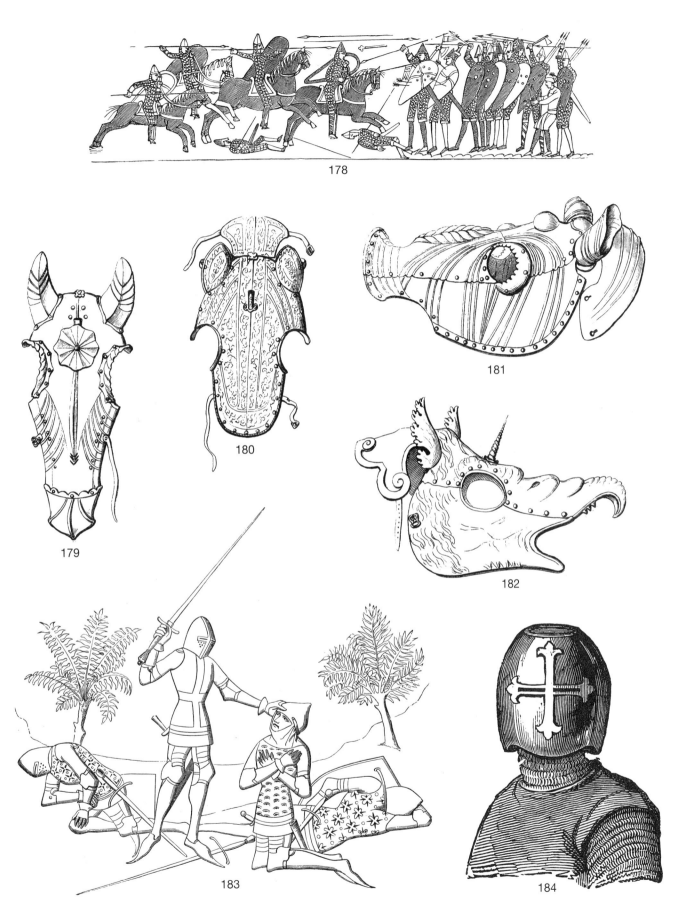

178. Battle of Hastings. 179–182. Various English champfreins. 183. Conferring knighthood on the field of battle, 13th century. 184. Helmet, 13th century.

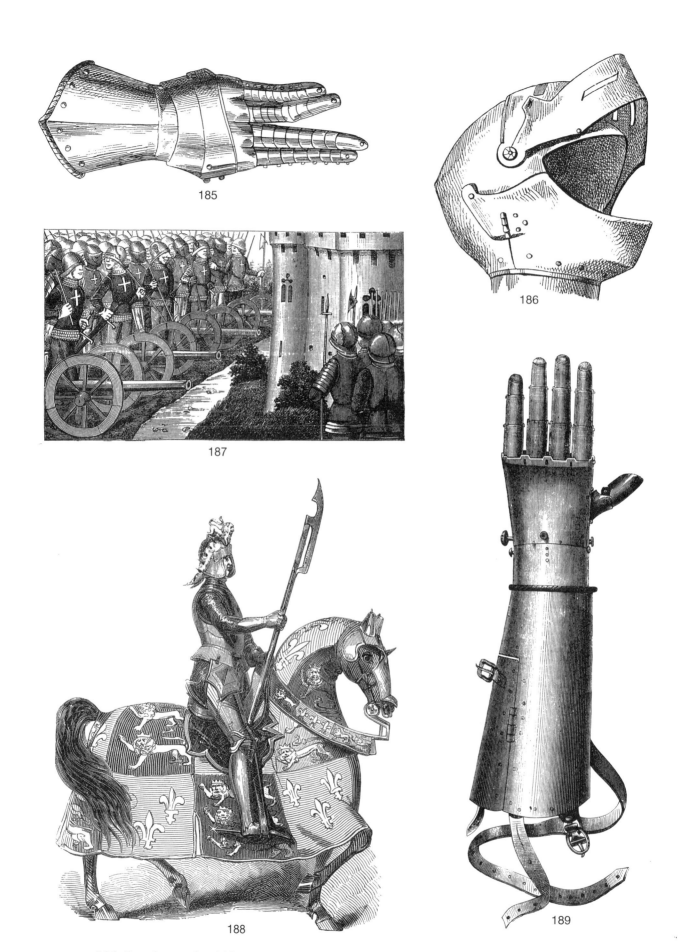

185. French gauntlet, 15th century. 186. French helmet, 15th century. 187. "How the Comte de Foix took strong places in Guienne," 1484. 188. Henry VI, 1450. 189. Gauntlet.

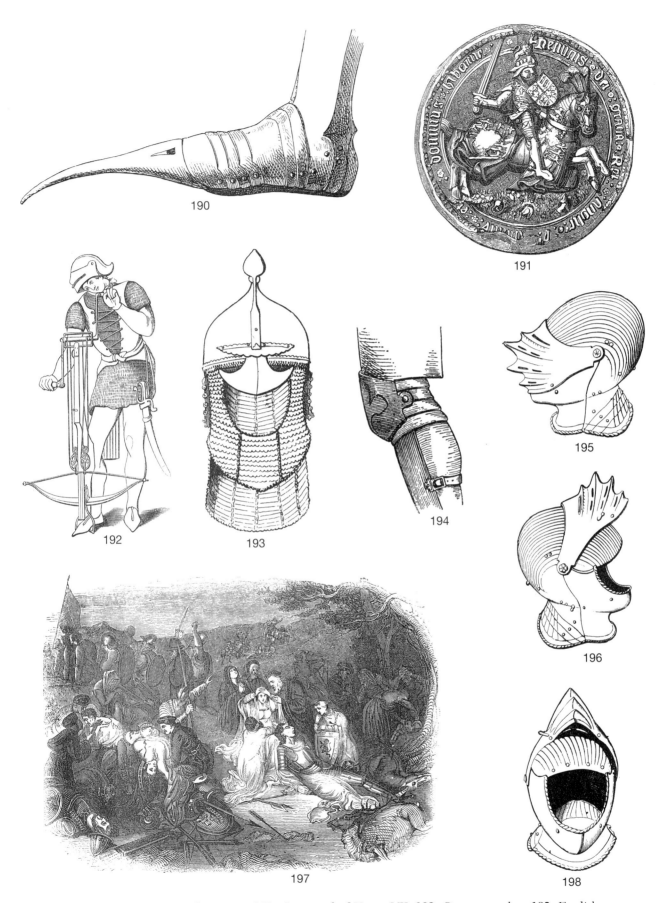

190. Solleret, 14th century. 191. Great seal of Henry VII. 192. Genoese archer. 193. English jousting helmet, 14th century. 194. Genouillere, 13th century. 195, 196, 198. English helmets, 15th century. 197. Field of the Battle of Chevy Chase.

199, 201. Bills, 14th–15th century. 200. Sword of Isabella the Catholic. 202. Seal of the
Commune of Soissons. 203. Breastplate of the time of Henry VIII. 204. Tournament armor.
205. Spanish helmet, 16th century. 206. Ballista, 14th century.

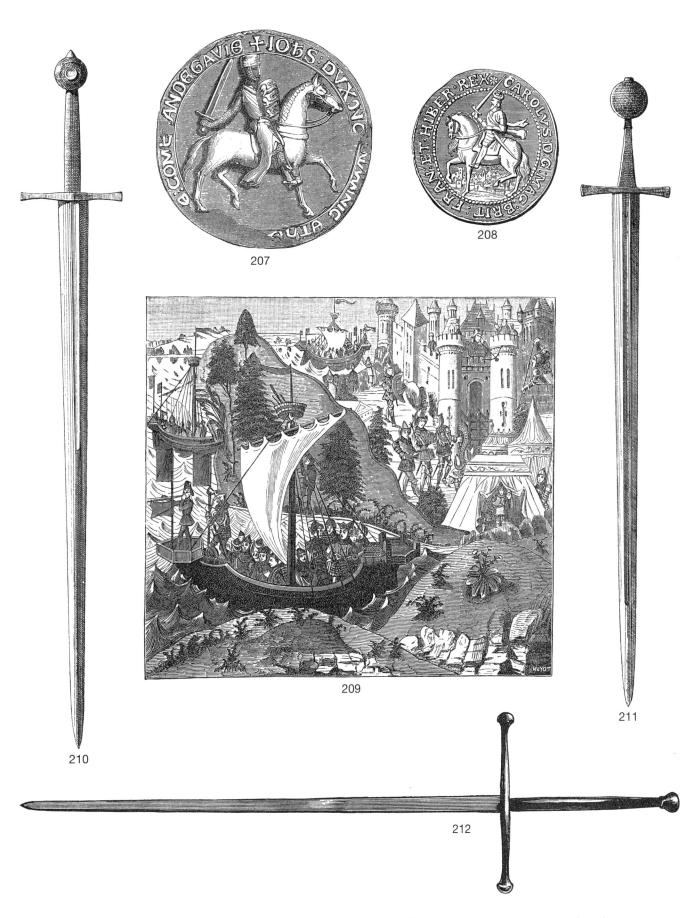

207. Great seal of King John. **208.** Oxford crown. **209.** Richard Coeur-de-Lion and Duke of Normandy. **210, 211.** Medieval European swords. **212.** Medieval two-handed sword.

213. Knights. **214.** Soldier of the time of Philippe le Bel. **215.** Knight of the Order of Rhodes. **216.** Knight in complete armor, 1590. **217.** Helmet, 1645. **218.** Arquebusier, 16th century.

219. Suit of armor with Lamboys. 220. Teutonic knight, 1585. 221. Tilting helmet of the time of Henry VII.
222. Robert Chamberlain, esquire to Henry V. 223. Tournament armor. 224. Tilting lance, 16th century.

225. Polish knight, 15th century. 226. French helmet, 15th century. 227. Richard Nevil, Earl of Warwick. 228. Military costume in the time of Henry VIII. 229. French gauntlet, 15th century. 230. Battering ram. 231. Helmet, 15th century.

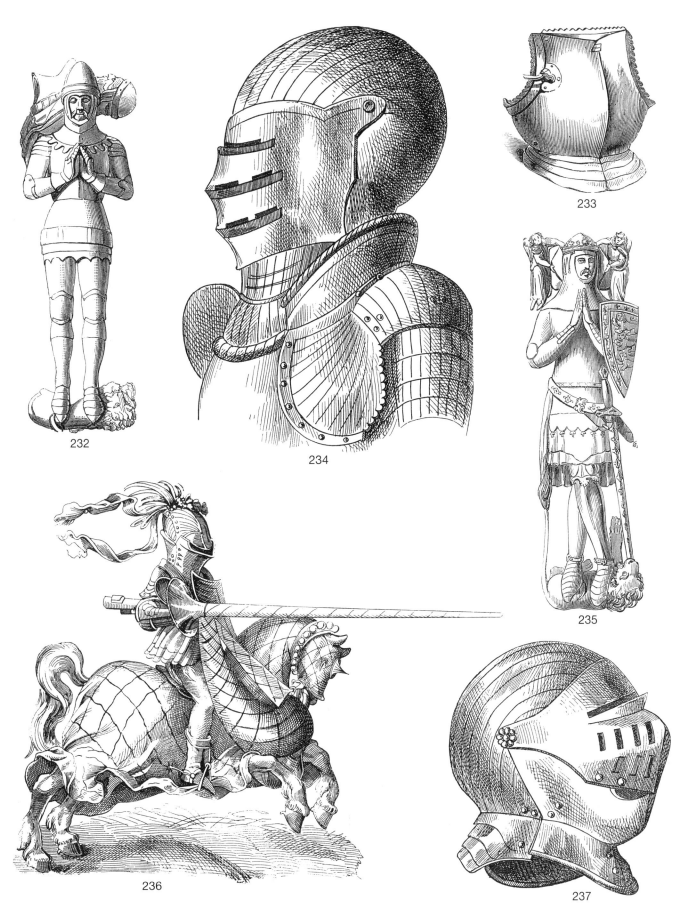

232. Effigy of Michael de la Pole, Earl of Suffolk. 233. Breastplate of the time of Henry VIII.
234. Helmet, 13th century. 235. John of Eltham. 236. Knight. 237. French helmet, 15th century.

238. Seal of the Lord of Corbeil. 239. Great seal of Henry V. 240, 246. Avantailes, 1203.
241. French basinet, 14th century. 242. Plumet helmet. 243, 245. Medieval European
swords. 244. Leg piece. 247. English crossbow, 15th century.

248. French gauntlet, 15th century. 249. Battle of Barnet. 250. English ships of war, 15th century. 251. Knight, 9th century.

252. Garde-brace, 15th century. 253. Soldiers in battle. 254. Sir Horace Vere. 255. Pikeman, 1635.
256. French helmet, 15th century. 257. Great seal of Richard I. 258. Civic guard of Ghent.

259

261

260

262

259. Knights in battle. 260. Helmet, shield, and saddle of Henry V. 261. Knight fending off an attack, 15th century. 262. Arms from the tower armory.

263. Tournament armor. 264. Knight in battle. 265. Dagger with Moorish blade and Flemish handle, 14th century. 266. Tilting lance, 16th century. 267. Henry VIII. 268. Medieval European swords. 269. Mace, 13th century.

270. Archers, 14th century. 271. Fire arrows, 14th century. 272. Knight in war harness.
273. Knight of Death, 1513. 274. Suit of puffed and engraved armor, 1510.

275, 277. Bills, 14th–15th century. 276. Man-at-arms, 11th century. 278. Great seal of Henry VIII. 279. Ordeal combat or duel. 280. James I. 281. Beheaded knight holding his fleshless head, 1562.